i can cook

fabulous fun for kids in the kitchen

recipes by
Sally Brown & Kate Morris

hamlyn

KATY SAYS
I hope you have fun
making these recipes!

An Hachette UK Company
www.hachette.co.uk

First published in Great Britain in 2010 by
Hamlyn, a division of Octopus Publishing Group Ltd
Carmelite House
50 Victoria Embankment
London
EC4Y 0DZ
www.octopusbooks.co.uk

ISBN 978-0-600-62206-2

A CIP catalogue record for this book is available from the British Library

Printed and bound in China

11

i can cook logo © Endemol UK plc 2009.
i can cook is a trade mark of Endemol UK plc. i can cook is produced by
Initial (part of Endemol UK) for the BBC

Series Consultants and Co-Devisers: Kate Morris and Sally Brown
Recipes by Kate Morris and Sally Brown

Notes

Standard level spoon measures are used in all recipes:

1 tablespoon = one 15 ml spoon

1 teaspoon = one 5 ml spoon

Ovens should be preheated to the specified temperature. If using a fan-
assisted oven, follow the manufacturer's instructions for adjusting the time
and temperature.

Medium eggs have been used throughout.

We recognise that many parents are choosing to avoid nuts and nut
products so most of the recipes in this selection do not include nuts (or
they may be added as an optional extra). Always be aware that
ingredients may have nut traces in them so check the packaging for
allergens if there is a risk of an allergic reaction.

About the authors

Sally Brown's passion for food began when she was very young.
During her childhood she regularly spent time in a commercial kitchen
as her parents were both restaurateurs. This provided Sally with an early,
valuable understanding of food preparation, hygiene, ingredients and
flavours. When she discovered that her own children were keen at 18
months old to join in the preparation of the family meal it inspired her
to set up a children's cooking business in 2000. In 2003 she was joined
by Kate Morris and together they offer cooking classes for children and
provide consultancy services to the media, local authorities, educational
settings, kitchen equipment manufacturers, retailers, supermarkets
and charities.

Kate Morris is a trained teacher with a B. Ed. (Hons) in Home
Economics. After a spell teaching in London she worked as a staff and
freelance writer for national home interest magazines. Kate spent her
two children's pre-school years cooking with them and realised that she
was one of a small minority of parents confident to do so. In 2003 she
joined forces with Sally, developing the skills and nutrition based strategy
for the cook school project they launched in 2003 with an emphasis on
real food education for both the children and their adult companions.

Contents

Introduction

Welcome to i can cook. We really hope you find this book helpful and fun to use.

Our i can cook philosophy is pretty simple. We firmly believe that children can do the cooking themselves rather than just watching or helping. If a young child can hold a paintbrush or cut paper with nursery scissors then it's easy for them to grease a cooking container with a pastry brush or cut up ingredients with scissors. That is why these recipes have been developed to be made easily with little or no adult help. Children learn about real food skills in this way and discover a wide variety of ingredients. In creating these recipes, and watching lots of excited children cooking them, we have also picked up a few hints and tips that we would like to share with you.

Getting started

The good news is, our recipes don't use long lists of ingredients so you will have most things to hand already, plus you really don't need any special equipment in order to get your kids into the kitchen. You should be ready to roll with what's already in your kitchen cupboards – with perhaps just the addition of an optional extra or two to add to the fun.

So, what is your little chef's workstation going to look like? Their preparation surface needs to be at their height to allow them to stand to cook – a painting or picnic table works well, for example. This means their feet are firmly planted on the floor and there is no risk of them toppling off a chair as they concentrate on mixing or snipping. You can sit beside them on a stool to talk and watch. A **big work mat** on top of the table works very well – it helps your chef to keep their space clear as they cook and you can be sure the surface is really clean as the mat can be washed in very hot water or even a dishwasher. If the mat is slippery, you can place a damp piece of kitchen roll underneath to help it stay in place.

You don't want to be left with all the clearing up, so make the preparation and washing up part of the fun too and help children learn good habits right from the start. On this note, get them into the habit of wearing an apron – less washing for you, and less chance of nasties in the cake mix.

Kitchen kit

Here are a few things we have found that make life a little easier:

• A **multi-purpose grater** (see above), which has a suction facility to stick it to the table, is a great tool for kids to use. You can also use other types of grater but be very careful of little fingers.

• We try to **avoid using sharp knives** and often use **scissors** to cut up ingredients such as cooked bacon and spring onions. Choose standard metal-bladed nursery scissors and keep them only for food use. And you can teach your child our rhyme as you cook – 'remember, when using scissors everyone knows, it's best to point them at your toes!'. When you do need to prepare something for your i can cook chef using a sharp knife, if cutting a lemon in half, for example, remember that your child is learning from you so use a chopping board and explain how sharp the knife is.

• Siliconised **baking paper on the baking tray** helps stop the food from sticking as it cooks in the oven. It also makes clearing up much easier! Sometimes a little oil is useful as well. Olive oil is usually specified where it adds flavour too.

• Where a **mixing bowl** is needed a 1 or 1.5 litre capacity is big enough for the i can cook chef to get their hands into the mixtures and is large enough to hold the small quantities they make.

• Many of the recipes use **spoons as a measure** – either a teaspoon (5 ml), a dessert spoon (10ml) or a tablespoon (15 ml). Unless the recipe says otherwise, the measure is level.

• If the measure is a ½ **cup** or full cup, this is the American measure (225 ml), and can often be found on small measuring jugs along with the millilitre measures.

- If an ingredient is to be weighed then old-fashioned **balance scales** allow the chef to actually hold the weights in their hands then see the pans levelling when the ingredient matches the weight needed – great fun.

- **Oven temperatures** are given for fan ovens, static electric ovens and a gas setting. Cooking times may vary depending on your oven and the material of the container you are using. For example, a metal casserole will heat up quicker than a china one, and a china one will hold its heat longer than a metal one – this can affect the cooking time. Use the recipe temperature and time as a guide but keep an eye on things just in case yours cook quicker.

- Where **eggs** are specified they are always medium size. Try to have more to hand than the recipe states so you always have a spare.

- Where **fresh vegetables,** fruit and herbs are used, always wash and then drain on a clean tea towel before using in a recipe. This is a good job for your chef to do.

I did it!

As young as three there are all sorts of skills your little chef already has, from drawing shapes with a pencil to placing pieces in a jigsaw. You may not have related these to cooking – but you will be amazed by what your child can do with your help and encouragement. We have developed these recipes with those skills in mind so relax and let them have a go.

The first time your child makes a recipe themselves, you may find they need quite a bit of help understanding the sequence and learning to handle the ingredients, but gradually you can assist less and watch more. As they prepare ingredients and put recipes together, your child will develop lots of other skills as they learn.

Cooking terms and techniques

- **Top and Tail** – This means when we take the ends off something like a spring onion or green bean leaving us with the bit we want to use in the recipe.

- **Tickling** – When we rub butter and flour together between our fingers and thumb to make a crumbly texture.

- **'Wet' and 'dry' bowl** – This is when we keep the wet ingredients like egg/oil in one mixing bowl and the dry ingredients such as flour and sugar in a different mixing bowl.

- **Two-spoon method** – Often used for muffin and cake mixtures this needs some coordination but gets easier with practice! Using two spoons, load some mixture on to one spoon and then use the back of the other spoon to push it off into the cooking container.

- **'Pop' a pepper** – Put a whole pepper on the work mat with the stalk facing up. Place both thumbs on the top where the stalk is, then push down into the middle of the pepper and the pepper will 'pop'. It can then be pulled apart and the stalk and core removed.

- **Kneading** – This is a push and pull stretching action when making bread. We like to pull the dough out like butterfly wings then fold it in half and turn, then keep repeating until the dough is really smooth. Add a little more flour to the surface if it gets too sticky.

- **Breaking an egg** – Hold onto the handle of a cup with one hand and the egg with the other. Hit the egg on to the edge of the cup and tap a few times. Listen to the sound change when the shell cracks. Then carefully use both thumbs to open the egg. Empty it into the cup.

Safety first

Cooking together is about having fun, but it's still important that you point out any potential dangers in the kitchen.

- Keep sharp knives well out of reach and out of sight and explain why you have to use some other tools for the time being.

- All the i can cook recipes have been devised to avoid use of the hob and are baked in the oven. You may need to melt some butter for a recipe but this can be put to one side and allowed to cool a little before your child starts using it.

- Always use an oven glove to put things in and out of the oven – this helps establish the rules for when your chef is old enough to do it themselves.

Eating well

Eating well means having the energy to run around and play, the energy bodies need to grow and mend – these are health messages children can understand. We like to sit down at the table and eat a meal together, and to join in the fun of trying new foods.

The recipes in this book have been developed to offer a range of nutritious main courses, both with or without meat, filling but balanced desserts, healthy snacks and a few sweet treats for once in a while. Young children need healthy snacks to keep them going. Only a couple of the i can cook recipes include added salt.

All the recipes have suggested portion sizes and serving suggestions. The recommended portion size is suitable for most children up to six years old and we have tried to suggest accompaniments to add balance to the meal, such as steamed green vegetables with a savoury main or a glass of diluted fruit juice with a snack. You can achieve a healthy balance by choosing a wide range of fruit and vegetables through the week. If your child doesn't like something the first time, don't give up – keep trying, with

just a little of the new food, and don't comment if they do or do not eat it. We don't insist on a clean plate – if your child isn't hungry then let them leave it as bribing children to finish their meal may disrupt their natural appetite.

A great way of involving children in food, and helping them understand what they are putting into their bodies, is to pick or grow an ingredient or two. It's amazing what you can grow even in a small space and some ingredients – herbs, for example – don't need an outdoor space at all. It really adds to the fun if you can grow something your child then uses to cook with, and makes an enormous difference to their understanding of where all those plastic-wrapped things in the supermarket really come from.

And finally, no recipe is meant to be followed to the letter. If something isn't in season or you can't find it, try an alternative. Tinned or frozen fruit or vegetables are a great option. That way you are helping your child to be a true i can cook chef.

Hand-washing song

Hey everybody, it's time to wash your hands and get your aprons on

Roll up your sleeves, give your hands a wash, with Slippy Dippy Soap, Splish Splash Splosh.

Cooking is fun but it can be mucky, So put your apron on to stop your clothes getting yucky

Have you done your hands?
YES!
Washed and dried?
YES!
Sleeves rolled up?
YES!
Apron Tied?
YES!

Let's take a look in the cookery book

What can you do?
I CAN COOK!

Before cooking, wash your hands and put an apron on

i can cook

Lunch

Cheese & vegetable pasties

These pasties taste great with some fresh tomatoes.

Ingredients
- flour for dusting
- half a 375 g pack puff pastry
- 4 spinach leaves
- 30 g Cheddar cheese, grated
- pinch of ground nutmeg
- 2 rounded teaspoons ratatouille (we used tinned)
- small bowl of water

Equipment
- workmat
- scales
- tin-opener (for adult use)
- 2 teaspoons
- flour dredger
- rolling pin
- large cutter or small plate (about 9 cm diameter)
- mixing bowl
- fork
- pastry brush
- baking tray
- baking paper
- oven gloves (for adult use)

Makes 2

What to do

1 Line the baking tray with baking paper.

KATY SAYS
If you buy fresh ready-made puff pastry, you can put any that's left over into the freezer for next time.

2 Sprinkle the workmat with flour from the dredger and roll out the puff pastry. Use the cutter to cut 4 circles into the pastry (or cut around the plate 4 times). Place 2 of the pastry circles on the baking tray.

3 Tear the spinach up into the bowl. Add most of the cheese, a pinch of nutmeg and the ratatouille and mix it all together.

4 Prick all the pastry circles with a fork. Spoon the mixture on to the centre of the 2 pastry circles on the baking tray.

5 Use the pastry brush to brush water around the edges of the filled pastry circles, like an island, and stick the remaining 2 pastry circles on top of each. Sprinkle more water on top and add the remaining grated cheese.

6 You'll need to ask an adult for help with this part. Place in a preheated oven, 200°C fan, 220°C, Gas Mark 7, for around 15 minutes, or until puffed up and golden.

Once the Cheese and Vegetable Pasties have cooled down a little, you can eat them!

Easy peasy pizza

Eat your pizza with some cucumber sticks or salad.

Serves 1

Ingredients
- 75 g self-raising flour
- 10 g soft butter
- 30 ml milk
- 4 cherry tomatoes
- 1 sprig fresh rosemary
- 5 green grapes
- 25 g Red Leicester or Cheddar cheese, grated
- pinch of pepper

Equipment
- workmat
- scales
- measuring jug
- grater
- 2 mixing bowls
- fork
- flour dredger
- scissors
- dessertspoon
- baking tray
- baking paper
- oven gloves (for adult use)

What to do

1 Line the baking tray with baking paper.

2 Put the flour and the butter in a bowl and rub them together with your fingers until the mixture becomes like crumbs. Add the milk (you may not need it all) and stir into a dough with the fork, then make the dough into a ball shape with your hands.

3 Dust some flour on the workmat and put the ball of dough on top. Flatten it with your hand into a pizza base, then place it on the baking tray.

KATY SAYS
When rubbing the flour and butter together, just imagine that you are tickling the mixture!

4 Put the tomatoes in a clean bowl and chop them up using clean scissors. (Remember, when using scissors, 'everyone knows, it's best to point them at your toes'!) Spoon the chopped tomatoes on to the pizza base.

5 Pull the leaves off the rosemary stalk and sprinkle them over the tomatoes. Add a pinch of pepper and put the grapes on top.

6 Sprinkle the grated cheese over the top. You'll need to ask an adult for help with this part. Place in a preheated oven, 200°C fan, 220°C, Gas Mark 7, for 10–15 minutes.

Once the Easy Peasy Pizza has cooled down a little, you can eat it!

Frittata

Serve the frittata with cherry tomatoes for a healthy lunch.

Ingredients
- sunflower or vegetable oil for greasing
- 100 g cooked potatoes (we used tinned)
- 1 spring onion
- 2 asparagus spears
- 2 heaped tablespoons frozen peas
- 5 fresh mint leaves, torn into small pieces
- 2 level tablespoons grated Parmesan cheese
- 2 eggs
- pinch of pepper

Equipment
- workmat
- scales
- tin-opener (for adult use)
- tablespoon
- pastry brush
- greaseproof bag
- rolling pin
- mixing bowl
- scissors
- cup
- fork
- ovenproof dish (about 400 ml capacity)
- baking tray
- oven gloves (for adult use)

What to do

1 Brush the inside of the ovenproof dish with the oil and put it on the baking tray.

KATY SAYS
'Topping and tailing' the spring onion means snipping off both ends.

2 Put the potatoes in a greaseproof bag and use a rolling pin to bash them until they are crushed into small pieces. (If you don't have a greaseproof bag, you can do this in a large bowl, using the end of a rolling pin to crush the potatoes.) Empty the crushed potatoes into the bowl.

3 'Top and tail' the spring onion and cut it into small pieces using clean scissors. Chop up the asparagus with the scissors. (Remember, when using scissors, 'everyone knows, it's best to point them at your toes'!) Add the spring onion, asparagus, peas, mint leaves and grated Parmesan to the bowl, and stir it all together.

4 Break the 2 eggs, one at a time, into the cup and beat lightly with a fork. Pour the beaten eggs into the mixing bowl and add a pinch of pepper. Stir until all of the ingredients are mixed together. Pour the mixture into the dish.

5 You'll need to ask an adult for help with this part. Place in a preheated oven, 180°C fan, 200°C, Gas Mark 6, for 15–20 minutes, or until completely set.

Once the Frittata has cooled down slightly, you can eat it!

Baked courgette with Parmesan

It's lovely to eat the courgette with sliced, fresh tomatoes.

Ingredients

- sunflower or vegetable oil for greasing
- 1 rasher cooked bacon
- 1 medium courgette
- 1 heaped tablespoon natural yogurt
- 25 g feta cheese
- 1 rounded tablespoon grated Parmesan cheese
- 1 egg
- pinch of pepper

Equipment

- workmat
- scales
- tablespoon
- grater
- pastry brush
- scissors
- small bowl
- cup
- fork
- ovenproof dish (about 400 ml capacity)
- baking tray
- oven gloves (for adult use)

Serves 2

What to do

1 Brush the inside of the oven-proof dish with oil and put it on the baking tray.

2 Cut up the bacon using clean scissors. (Remember, when using scissors, 'everyone knows, it's best to point them at your toes'!)

KATY SAYS
Ask an adult to cook the bacon rasher for you, or you can buy ready-cooked bacon.

3 Carefully grate the courgette and put it in the ovenproof dish. Scatter over the bacon pieces.

4 Put the yogurt in the bowl, then crumble in the feta cheese with your fingers and mix it together with the fork. Add the grated Parmesan cheese and a pinch of pepper, and stir it again.

5 Crack the egg into the cup and whisk it with the fork. Then add it to the yogurt mix and stir. Pour the egg and yogurt mixture on top of the courgette and bacon in the dish.

6 You'll need to ask an adult for help with this part. Place in a preheated oven, 160°C fan, 180°C, Gas Mark 4, for 20–25 minutes.

Once the Baked Courgette with Parmesan has cooled down a little, you can eat it!

Katy's lasagne

Serve the lasagne with cucumber sticks or a fresh green salad.

Serves 2

Ingredients
- 1 teaspoon olive oil, plus some for greasing
- 200 g chopped tinned tomatoes
- 1 sheet fresh lasagne
- 30 g (¼ ball) mozzarella cheese
- 100 g ricotta cheese
- 6 fresh basil leaves
- 1 slice of ham
- pinch of pepper

Equipment
- workmat
- scales
- tin-opener (for adult use)
- 2 teaspoons
- pastry brush
- small bowl
- fork
- ovenproof dish with lid (about 400 ml capacity)
- baking tray
- oven gloves (for adult use)

What to do

1 Brush the inside of the ovenproof dish with olive oil.

2 Put a thin layer of chopped tomatoes and juice in the bottom of the dish. Tear the lasagne sheet and put half of it in the dish, hiding the tomatoes. Then add another layer of tomatoes and juice on top.

3 In the bowl, squash the mozzarella cheese using the back of a fork and sprinkle half of it over the tomatoes. Using the 2-spoon method with the 2 teaspoons, add half the ricotta cheese over the top. Then tear 3 of the basil leaves and add to the dish.

KATY SAYS
This is also delicious when made with tinned fish instead of ham

4 Tear up the piece of ham and put half of this on top of the cheese and basil, then sprinkle over a pinch of pepper.

5 Repeat the layer process with the remaining ingredients: lasagne, tomatoes, basil, ham, ricotta and mozzarella. (Make sure that you put the ricotta and mozzarella cheese on last.) Add a final pinch of pepper on the top with a sprinkle of olive oil.

6 Put the lid on the dish, then lift it on to the baking tray. You'll need to ask an adult for help with this part. Place in a preheated oven, 160°C fan, 180°C, Gas Mark 4, for 10 minutes with the lid on, and then a further 10 minutes without the lid or until completely cooked through.

Once the Katy's Lasagne has cooled down slightly, you can eat it!

Savoury hot pot

Eat this dish with some lovely steamed vegetables.

Ingredients

- 1 spring onion
- 30 g tinned cannellini beans (rinsed and drained)
- 1 cabbage leaf
- 2 heaped tablespoons tinned chopped tomatoes
- 2 cooked sausages (ask an adult to do this for you)
- large pinch of stock powder
- 75 ml water
- a few stalks of fresh thyme
- ½ teaspoon wholegrain mustard
- pinch of pepper

Equipment

- workmat
- scales
- measuring jug
- tin-opener (for adult use)
- tablespoon
- teaspoon
- scissors
- sieve
- ovenproof dish with lid (about 400 ml capacity)
- baking tray
- oven gloves (for adult use)

What to do

1 'Top and tail' the spring onion and cut it into small pieces using clean scissors. (Remember, when using scissors, 'everyone knows, it's best to point them at your toes'!) Put it in the ovenproof dish together with the cannellini beans.

2 Tear the cabbage leaf into small pieces and add them to the dish, then cover with the chopped tomatoes. Add the cooked sausages to the top.

3 Mix the stock powder with the water in the measuring jug. Strip the leaves off the stalks of thyme with your fingers, then add them along with the mustard to the stock. Pour it over the ingredients in the ovenproof dish and finish with a pinch of pepper.

4 Put the lid on the dish, then lift it on to the baking tray. You'll need to ask an adult for help with this part. Place in a pre-heated oven, 140°C fan, 160°C, Gas Mark 3, for about 20 minutes, or until completely cooked through.

KATY SAYS
Try to find some curly kale cabbage for this recipe.

Once the Savoury Hot Pot has cooled down a little, you can eat it!

Magic mini fishcakes

These are nice to eat with some steamed French beans.

Ingredients
- 2 stalks fresh curly parsley
- 105 g tin pink or red salmon (boneless)
- 1 spring onion
- 1 slice day-old bread
- 1 rounded tablespoon tomato ketchup
- olive oil, for brushing
- pinch of pepper

Equipment
- workmat
- tin-opener (for adult use)
- tablespoon
- mixing bowl
- scissors
- fork
- multi-purpose grater
- pastry brush
- baking tray
- baking paper
- oven gloves (for adult use)

Serves 2

What to do

1 Line the baking tray with baking paper.

2 Put the parsley in the bowl and chop up with clean scissors. (Remember, when using scissors, 'everyone knows, it's best to point them at your toes'!)

3 Add the salmon to the parsley and mix it together with the fork.

KATY SAYS
I like making these with tinned tuna too!

4 'Top and tail' the spring onion and cut it into small pieces using clean cissors, then add it to the salmon.

5 Tear up the bread and carefully grate it into breadcrumbs. Add a tablespoon of the bread-crumbs to the salmon mixture, then a tablespoon of ketchup and a pinch of pepper. Divide the mixture into 2 parts and roll them into balls.

6 Roll the balls in the remaining breadcrumbs until they are covered, put them on the baking tray and squash them slightly with your hands. Using the pastry brush, brush oil on top.

7 You'll need to ask an adult for help with this part. Place in a preheated oven, 200°C fan, 220°C, Gas Mark 7, for 10–15 minutes.

Once your Magic Mini Fishcakes have cooled down a little, you can eat them!

Baked spaghetti

Serve with a little grated cheese sprinkled on top.

Serves 2

Ingredients
- 1 spring onion
- 2 sun-dried tomatoes
- 1 rasher cooked crispy bacon (you can buy ready-cooked bacon)
- 3 black olives
- 50 g dried spaghetti
- 125 ml water
- 125 ml tinned chopped tomatoes
- large pinch of stock powder
- pinch of paprika

Equipment
- workmat
- scales
- measuring jug
- tin-opener (for adult use)
- scissors
- ovenproof dish with lid (about 400 ml capacity)
- baking tray
- oven gloves (for adult use)

What to do

1 'Top and tail' the spring onion and cut it into small pieces using clean scissors. (Remember, when using scissors, 'everyone knows, it's best to point them at your toes'!)

2 Cut up the sun-dried tomatoes with the scissors, and put the spring onion and sun-dried tomatoes in the ovenproof dish. Tear up the bacon and olives and add them to the dish.

KATY SAYS
You could try making this with other types of cooked meat.

3 Snap the spaghetti so that it fits into your dish and add to the other ingredients.

4 Pour in the water and chopped tomatoes, then add the stock powder and paprika.

5 Put the lid on the dish and place it on the baking tray. You'll need to ask an adult for help with this part. Put it in a preheated oven, 200°C fan, 220°C, Gas Mark 7, for 25 minutes, or until the spaghetti is cooked through.

Once the Baked Spaghetti has cooled down a little, you can eat it!

Fish triple decker

Eat this with French beans or another green vegetable.

Serves 1-2

Ingredients

- olive oil for greasing
- 2 small mushrooms
- 4 black olives without stones
- 2 stalks fresh curly parsley
- 1 haddock fillet or similar white fish fillet
- tomato ketchup
- 1 rounded tablespoon sweetcorn
- 1 slice day-old bread
- 25 g Cheddar cheese, grated
- pinch of pepper

Equipment

- workmat
- scales
- tablespoon
- multi-purpose grater
- pastry brush
- cup
- scissors
- mixing bowl
- baking tray
- baking paper
- oven gloves (for adult use)

What to do

1 Line the baking tray with baking paper and brush the paper with oil.

2 Tear up the mushrooms and olives. Put the parsley in the cup and chop it up using clean scissors. (Remember, when using scissors, 'everyone knows, it's best to point them at your toes'!)

3 Place the fish on the baking tray. Squirt tomato ketchup on top of the fish and spread it with a spoon to cover the top of the fish. Scatter the olives, mushrooms, parsley and sweetcorn on top.

4 Prepare the breadcrumb topping by tearing up the bread and grating it carefully with a grater. In the bowl, mix together the cheese and pepper with the bread-crumbs and then tip them over the fish.

5 You'll need to ask an adult for help with this part. Place the baking tray in a preheated oven, 180°C fan, 200°C, Gas Mark 6, for about 20 minutes, or until completely cooked through.

Once your Fish Triple Decker has cooled down slightly, you can eat it!

KATY SAYS
Whether this serves 1 or 2 depends on the size of your fish fillet.

Baked risotto

Enjoy this risotto with some of the leftover pepper, vegetables or salad.

Serves 1–2

Ingredients

- 1 small red pepper (you'll only use half)
- 1 tablespoon olive oil
- 50 g arborio risotto rice
- 1 spring onion
- 1 heaped tablespoon frozen or fresh peas
- 2 small mushrooms
- 50 g cooked chicken (ready-cooked or leftovers)
- 125 ml warm water
- large pinch of stock powder

Equipment

- workmat
- scales
- measuring jug
- tablespoon
- scissors
- ovenproof dish with lid (about 400 ml capacity)
- baking tray
- oven gloves (for adult use)

What to do

1 'Pop' the pepper by pushing in the stalk with your thumbs until it disappears inside (see page 32), then tear the pepper in half. Remove the seeds from inside one half of the pepper and tear it up into smaller pieces.

2 Pour the oil into the ovenproof dish, then add the rice and the pieces of red pepper.

3 'Top and tail' the spring onion and cut it into small pieces using clean scissors. (Remember, when using scissors, 'everyone knows, it's best to point them at your toes'!) Add the pieces of spring onion and the peas to the dish.

KATY SAYS
You could use a green or orange pepper instead of the red one.

4 Tear up the mushrooms and the cooked chicken with your fingers and add them to the dish.

5 Pour in the warm water and add the stock powder. Stir with the spoon.

6 Put the lid on the dish and place it on the baking tray. You'll need to ask an adult for help with this part. Place the baking tray in a preheated oven, 180°C fan, 200°C, Gas Mark 6, for 20–25 minutes, or until the rice is completely cooked.

Once your Baked Risotto has cooled down slightly, you can eat it!

Cheesy chicken

The filled pepper half goes very well with peas.

Ingredients

- olive oil for greasing
- 2 cherry tomatoes
- 2 fresh basil leaves
- 1 fresh pepper
- 50 g cooked chicken (ask an adult to do this for you)
- 25 g mozzarella cheese
- 1 level tablespoon grated cheese, such as Cheddar or Parmesan
- pinch of pepper

Equipment

- workmat
- scales
- tablespoon
- pastry brush
- 2 small mixing bowls
- scissors
- fork
- baking tray
- baking paper
- oven gloves (for adult use)

What to do

1 Line the baking tray with baking paper and brush it with oil.

2 Chop up the cherry tomatoes in a bowl using clean scissors. (Remember, when using scissors, 'everyone knows, it's best to point them at your toes'!) Add the pepper, then tear up the basil and mix it all together.

3 'Pop' the fresh pepper by pushing in the stalk with your thumbs until you push it inside. Tear it in half with your thumbs and remove the seeds. Place half the pepper on the prepared baking tray with the open side up so it becomes a bowl.

4 Tear up the chicken and fill the pepper half. Put the cherry tomato mix on top, hiding the chicken.

5 Squash and break up the mozzarella cheese in a separate bowl with a fork. Put the squashed mozzarella cheese on top of the tomatoes, then sprinkle the pepper and grated cheese on top.

6 You'll need to ask an adult for help with this part. Place the baking tray in a preheated oven, 180°C fan, 200°C, Gas Mark 6, for about 20 minutes, or until completely cooked through.

Once the Cheesy Chicken has cooled down a little, you can eat it!

Baked bean soup

Serve this yummy soup with crusty bread.

Ingredients
- 3 heaped dessertspoons (about 60 g) tinned borlotti beans (rinsed and drained)
- 1 spring onion
- 1 stalk celery
- 3 dessertspoons (about 50 g) chopped cooked bacon (you can buy ready-cooked bacon)
- 1 clove garlic
- pinch of chilli flakes
- 1 heaped tablespoon tomato purée
- 250 ml water
- pinch of stock powder

Equipment
- workmat
- measuring jug
- dessertspoon
- scissors
- greaseproof paper bag
- rolling pin
- sieve
- tablespoon
- ovenproof dish with lid (about 400 ml capacity)
- baking tray
- oven gloves (for adult use)

What to do

1 Put the beans in the dish. You can give them a bit of a squash with the back of the spoon to loosen the skins – this will help thicken the soup.

2 'Top and tail' the spring onion and cut it up into small pieces using clean scissors. (Remember, when using scissors, 'everyone knows, it's best to point them at your toes'!) Cut up the celery stalk with the scissors (you might find you can snap the celery) and add the pieces to the dish. Add the chopped bacon.

3 Take the clove of garlic and 'top and tail' it with the scissors, then peel off the dry papery layer. Put the garlic in the bag and crush with the rolling pin. Use the dessertspoon to scoop out the crushed garlic and add it to the dish.

KATY SAYS
This tasty soup also counts towards your five a day.

4 Add the chilli flakes and tomato purée using the spoon. Add the water and stock powder, stir well and put the lid on.

5 Place the dish on the baking tray. You'll need to ask an adult for help with this part. Bake in a preheated oven, 160°C fan, 180°C, Gas Mark 4, for 25–30 minutes and stir well before serving.

Once your Baked Bean Soup has cooled down a little, you can eat it!

Spicy baked wraps

Enjoy these spicy wraps with some fresh salad.

Ingredients

- 1 spring onion
- 1 small salami sausage, cut into small chunks
- 3 tablespoons fresh podded broad beans (you can also use tinned broad beans)
- olive oil for greasing
- 1 flat bread wrap
- 50 g chopped tomatoes
- 25 g Cheddar cheese, grated
- pinch of paprika
- pinch of pepper

Equipment

- workmat
- scales
- tin-opener (for adult use)
- tablespoon
- scissors
- mixing bowl
- greaseproof paper bag
- rolling pin
- foil
- baking tray
- oven gloves (for adult use)

Serves 2

What to do

1 'Top and tail' the spring onion and cut it into small pieces using clean scissors. (Remember, when using scissors, 'everyone knows, it's best to point them at your toes'!) Put the spring onion and the salami in the bowl.

2 Remove the fresh beans from their pods by snapping the pod in half and pushing the beans out with your fingers. Put the beans in a greaseproof paper bag and bash them with a rolling pin to squash them. Add the squashed beans to the bowl. Add the pepper and paprika and stir it all together with the spoon.

3 Oil a piece of foil that's bigger than your wrap, place the wrap on top, then lift it on to the baking tray. Spread the chopped tomatoes all over the wrap like a pizza using the back of the spoon. Mark a line down the middle of the wrap with the edge of the spoon.

KATY SAYS
If you don't have a grease-proof paper bag, crush the beans in a bowl with the end of a rolling pin.

4 Spoon the bean mixture on to one side of the line you have drawn, and sprinkle the grated cheese on top. Fold the tomato side of the wrap over to make a parcel and fold the foil around it, scrunching it at the edges to seal the wrap inside.

5 You'll need to ask an adult for help with this part. Place the baking tray in a preheated oven, 180°C fan, 200°C, Gas Mark 6, for 15–20 minutes.

Once the Spicy Baked Wraps have cooled down a little, you can eat them!

Garlic chicken

Eat with cooked rice or pasta and green beans.

Ingredients
- 1 cooked chicken breast, skinned
- ¼ orange pepper
- 4 baby Anya or new potatoes
- 2 heaped tablespoons canned red kidney beans (rinsed and drained)
- 1 mini salami sausage
- 3 whole cloves garlic
- 1 level teaspoon cornflour or plain flour
- pinch of vegetable stock powder
- pinch of paprika
- ½ teaspoon yeast extract
- 125 ml water

Equipment
- workmat
- 2 measuring jugs
- tablespoon
- teaspoon
- scissors
- sieve
- ovenproof dish with lid (about 400 ml capacity)
- baking tray
- oven gloves (for adult use)

What to do

1 Place the ovenproof dish on the baking tray. Use clean scissors to cut the chicken into bite-sized pieces and then add them to the dish. (Remember, when using scissors, 'everyone knows, it's best to point them at your toes'!)

2 'Pop' your pepper by pushing in the stalk with your thumbs until it disappears inside (see page 32), then tear a quarter of it up and add to the dish. Put in the potatoes and kidney beans.

3 Use the scissors to cut up the mini salami, then add it with the cloves of garlic – you can leave them in their wrappings!

4 Make the flavoured stock by putting the flour, stock powder, paprika and yeast extract in a jug. Gradually add the water, mixing well. Pour enough stock mixture over the chicken and vegetables just to cover them, then put the lid on.

KATY SAYS
I love adding fresh herbs like thyme to my garlic chicken.

5 You'll need to ask an adult for help with this part. Bake in a preheated oven, 200°C fan, 220°C, Gas Mark 7, for 30 minutes or until the potatoes are cooked.

Once your Garlic Chicken has cooled down a little, you can eat it!

Boreks

It's good to eat these tasty bites with a mixed salad.

Serves 4

Ingredients
- 100 g feta cheese
- 1 heaped teaspoon (5–10 g) raisins or sultanas
- 20 g fresh flat leaf parsley
- 4 sheets filo pastry
- 50 g melted butter (ask an adult to melt it for you)
- pepper

Equipment
- workmat
- scales
- teaspoon
- mixing bowl
- scissors
- cup
- pastry brush
- baking tray
- baking paper
- oven gloves (for adult use)

What to do

1 Line the baking tray with baking paper.

2 Using your fingers, crumble the feta cheese into the bowl. Season with pepper. Add the raisins or sultanas and stir together with a spoon. Pinch all the long stalks off the parsley and chop the leaves with the scissors in the cup. (Remember, when using scissors, 'everyone knows, it's best to point them at your toes'!) Add the parsley to the bowl of cheese and raisins and mix them together.

KATY SAYS
See page 43 for step-by-step diagrams that show you how to fold a borek.

3 Take 1 piece of filo, brush some melted butter on one side and fold in half lengthways.

4 Put 2–3 heaped teaspoons of filling at one end and start to fold in triangles (see page 43), buttering the pastry as you go.

5 Place on the baking tray with the last fold at the bottom. Continue until all the filling is used – you should make 4 boreks.

now turn the page ▷

▷ continues from page 41

6 You'll need to ask an adult for help with this part. Bake in a preheated oven, 180°C fan, 200°C, Gas Mark 6, for about 20 minutes or until crisp and golden.

Once your Boreks have cooled down a little, you can eat them!

How to fold a borek

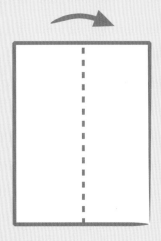

Step 1

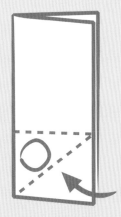

Step 2

Step 3

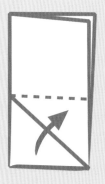

Step 4

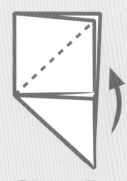

Step 5

Step 6

Step 7

KATY SAYS
Try adding pine nuts
instead of dried fruit for
a different texture.

Vegetable bhuna

Serve this tasty curry with rice or pasta.

Serves 2

Ingredients
- 2 spring onions
- ¼ fresh pepper
- 50 g (about 10) dwarf beans
- 4 baby sweetcorn
- 4 baby new potatoes
- 1 teaspoon Madras curry paste
- 125 ml tinned chopped tomatoes
- 125 ml water

Equipment
- workmat
- scales
- measuring jug
- tin-opener (for adult use)
- teaspoon
- scissors
- fork
- ovenproof dish with lid (about 400 ml capacity)
- baking tray
- oven gloves (for adult use)

What to do

1 'Top and tail' the spring onions and cut them into small pieces using clean scissors. (Remember, when using scissors, 'everyone knows, it's best to point them at your toes'!) Put them in the bottom of your ovenproof dish. Tear up or snip the fresh pepper and add that too.

2 Either pinch the tops off and snap the dwarf beans or cut them up, and add them to the cooking dish. Place the baby sweetcorn and the potatoes on top of the mixed vegetables.

3 Use the fork to mix the curry paste with the tinned tomatoes and pour on top of the vegetables. Top with the water just to cover, and put on the lid. Place the dish on a baking tray.

4 You'll need to ask an adult for help with this part. Place the dish in a preheated oven, 180°C fan, 200°C, Gas Mark 6, for 40 minutes or until the potatoes are cooked.

Once your **Vegetable Bhuna** has cooled down a little, you can eat it!

KATY SAYS
I sometimes use milk instead of water for a different flavour.

Vegetable spring rolls

Serve with extra dipping sauce for dunking the rolls in.

Ingredients

- vegetable oil for greasing
- 50 g coarsely grated carrot
- 50 g tinned cannellini beans (rinsed and drained)
- 50 g fresh bean shoots
- 1 spring onion
- ¼ red pepper
- 1 tablespoon chilli dipping sauce, plus extra to serve
- 8 sheets fresh filo pastry (we used fresh square-shaped filo)

Equipment

- workmat
- scales
- tin-opener (for adult use)
- grater
- tablespoon
- pastry brush
- 2 mixing bowls
- sieve
- kitchen paper
- fork
- scissors
- small bowl for oil
- baking tray
- baking paper
- oven gloves (for adult use)

Makes 4 rolls

What to do

1 Line the baking tray with baking paper and brush it with oil.

2 Put the grated carrot and beans in a bowl and mix together with the fork.

3 Rinse the bean shoots and dry using some kitchen paper, then put them in the other bowl and chop up with clean scissors. (Remember, when using scissors, 'everyone knows, it's best to point them at your toes'!) Add to the carrot and beans. 'Top and tail' the spring onion and cut it into small pieces with the scissors, then add these to the carrot and beans and mix.

KATY SAYS
See page 49 for step-by-step diagrams that show you how to fold a spring roll.

4 Either 'pop' the fresh pepper or cut it into small pieces and add to the other vegetables. Stir in the chilli dipping sauce.

5 Take out the sheets of filo pastry. Lay one sheet on a clean surface and dab it all over with oil. Place another piece on top and dab it with oil too. Turn the pastry with your hands so that a corner is pointing towards you (like a diamond).

6 Spoon on some of the filling near the corner nearest you. Fold this corner towards the centre and tuck it under the filling.

now turn the page

▷ continues from page 47

7 Fold the 2 outside corners in towards the middle so it looks like an envelope.

8 Dab with oil and then roll up the pastry to look like a sausage. Dab with more oil and put on the baking tray. Repeat until you have made 4. You'll need to ask an adult for help with this part. Place in a preheated oven, 200°C fan, 220°C, Gas Mark 7, for 15–20 minutes until crisp and golden.

Once your Vegetable Spring Rolls have cooled down a little, you can eat them!

How to fold a spring roll

Step 1

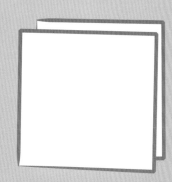

Step 2

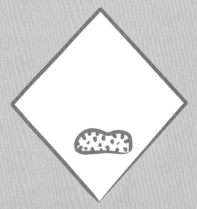

Step 3

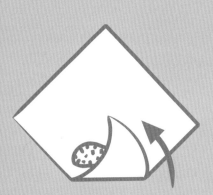

Step 4

Step 5

Step 6

KATY SAYS
You can use any leftover filo pastry to make some boreks (see pages 40–44).

Simple fish supper

Steamed broccoli goes very well with this fish dish.

Ingredients

- vegetable oil for greasing
- 1 spring onion
- 50 g soft cheese with garlic and herbs
- 1 teaspoon plain flour
- 125 ml milk
- 2 heaped tablespoons fresh or frozen peas
- 6 cherry tomatoes
- 1 white fish fillet, skinned
- 20 g melted butter (get an adult to melt it for you)
- 1 slice of thick, day-old bread

Equipment

- workmat
- scales
- measuring jug
- pastry brush
- scissors
- teaspoon
- fork
- mixing bowl
- tablespoon
- cup
- ovenproof dish (about 400 ml capacity)
- baking tray
- oven gloves (for adult use)

Serves 2

What to do

KATY SAYS
Instead of cutting the tomatoes with scissors, bashing the tomatoes in a greaseproof paper bag is lots of fun!

1 Brush the inside of the ovenproof dish with vegetable oil and place the ovenproof dish on the baking tray.

2 'Top and tail' the spring onion and cut it into small pieces using clean scissors. (Remember, when using scissors, 'everyone knows, it's best to point them at your toes'!) Put the pieces in the dish.

3 Squash the soft cheese in the cup with the plain flour and mix with a fork. Stir in the milk until it's smooth. Add the peas to the sauce.

4 Put the tomatoes in the measuring jug and chop them up with the scissors.

5 Cut the fish up with the scissors and put it in the dish. Pour the sauce you have made over the top. Add the chopped tomatoes.

6 Put the melted butter in a bowl. Tear the bread into chunks. Drop the bread into the butter so that each piece soaks up some butter, then put the bread on the top of your fish.

7 You'll need to ask an adult for help with this part. Place in a preheated oven, 180°C fan, 200°C, Gas Mark 6, for 20–25 minutes or until golden brown and the fish is cooked.

Once your Simple Fish Supper has cooled down a little, you can eat it!

crispy fish fingers

Eat your yummy fish fingers with chopped fresh tomatoes.

Serves 2

Ingredients

- vegetable oil for greasing
- 1 egg
- 1 slice day-old bread
- 2 tablespoons polenta (quick-cook, dried)
- pinch of pepper
- 3 tablespoons plain flour
- pinch of paprika
- 1 white fish fillet (skinned and boned)
- ½ lemon (ask an adult to cut this for you) or lemon juice

Equipment

- workmat
- tablespoon
- pastry brush
- 3 mixing bowls
- fork
- multi-purpose grater
- scissors
- baking tray
- baking paper
- oven gloves (for adult use)

What to do

1 Line the baking tray with baking paper and brush generously with vegetable oil.

2 Break the egg into one of the bowls and mix it well with the fork. This is going to stick the crunchy coating to the fish.

3 Using the grater, turn the slice of bread into breadcrumbs and put these in the second bowl. Add the polenta and pepper to the breadcrumbs and mix together with the spoon. This is your crunchy coating.

KATY SAYS
I like to eat fish twice a week as it's good for me and tastes great.

4 Put the plain flour and paprika in the third bowl and mix. This is the first layer of coating on your fish.

5 Arrange the bowls in order with the flour, then the egg, then the polenta mix.

6 Cut the fish fillet into strips about 3 cm wide using clean scissors. (Remember, when using scissors, 'everyone knows, it's best to point them at your toes'!) Squeeze lemon juice all over the fish pieces.

7 In turn, roll each fish strip in the flour bowl, then the egg bowl, then the polenta mix bowl, then put it on the baking paper. Once all the pieces of fish are coated, drip more oil on top of them.

8 You'll need to ask an adult for help with this part. Place in a preheated oven, 200°C fan, 220°C, Gas Mark 7, for 10–12 minutes or until the fish is cooked through.

Once the Crispy Fish Fingers have cooled down a little, you can eat them!

Toad in the hole

Serve this main dish with green pepper strips.

Serves 2

Ingredients
- vegetable oil for greasing
- 1 egg
- 100 ml milk
- 5 dessertspoons plain flour
- 1 teaspoon wholegrain mustard
- 2 cooked chipolata sausages
- 4 cherry tomatoes

Equipment
- workmat
- measuring jug
- dessertspoon
- teaspoon
- pastry brush
- mixing bowl
- fork
- scissors
- ovenproof dish (about 400 ml capacity)
- baking tray
- oven gloves (for adult use)

What to do

1 Brush the inside of the ovenproof dish with vegetable oil and place the ovenproof dish on the baking tray.

2 Break the egg into the bowl and whisk it with the fork. Add the milk and mix well.

3 Add the flour to the bowl and use the fork to whisk it until you can see lots of bubbles! Make sure all the flour is mixed in. Add the mustard and mix again.

4 Use clean scissors to cut each of the sausages into 4. (Remember, when using scissors, 'everyone knows, it's best to point them at your toes'!) Put them in the dish.

5 Put the tomatoes in the measuring jug. Cut them up using the scissors and add them to the dish. Place the dish on the baking tray and pour the liquid in over the top of the sausages and tomatoes.

6 You'll need to ask an adult for help with this part. Place in a preheated oven, 200°C fan, 220°C, Gas Mark 7, for 15–20 minutes.

Once the Toad in the Hole has cooled down a little, you can eat it!

KATY SAYS
You can make individual portions by using ramekin dishes.

Sweetheart quiche

This quiche tastes nice with cucumber batons and mixed pepper strips.

Ingredients

- vegetable oil for greasing
- 60 g plain flour
- 30 g soft butter
- 3–4 teaspoons cold water
- 1 egg
- 2 dessertspoons milk
- 1 slice ham
- 1 stalk fresh parsley
- 1 dessertspoon tinned sweetcorn
- 15 g grated cheese
- pinch of pepper

Equipment

- workmat
- scales
- tin-opener (for adult use)
- teaspoon
- dessertspoon
- pastry brush
- mixing bowl
- fork
- flour dredger
- rolling pin
- 2 cups
- scissors
- small heart-shaped tin (about 11 cm at the widest point)
- baking tray
- oven gloves (for adult use)

What to do

1 Brush the inside of the heart-shaped tin with a very little oil.

2 Put the flour and butter in the bowl and rub them together with your fingers until the mixture becomes crumbly (just imagine you are tickling it!).

3 Add the water until the mixture sticks together to make a soft ball of dough. Sprinkle flour on your workmat, then roll the dough out with the rolling pin until it is bigger all round than the tin. Lift the pastry over the tin and push it into the shape. Trim with the rolling pin and put the tin in the fridge.

4 Use clean scissors to cut the ham into bite-sized pieces. In the cup, cut up the parsley leaves with the scissors. (Remember, when using scissors, 'everyone knows, it's best to point them at your toes'!) Now get your pastry case out of the fridge and put the ham, parsley and sweetcorn at the bottom.

5 Break the egg into the other cup and whisk with the fork. Add the milk and season with pepper. Pour the mixture into the pastry case – you may not be able to get it all in! Sprinkle with the cheese.

6 Place the tin on the baking tray. You'll need to ask an adult for help with this part. Place the quiche in a preheated oven, 180°C fan, 200°C, Gas Mark 6, for 20 minutes or until golden brown on top.

Once the Sweetheart Quiche has cooled down a little, you can eat it!

Sausage kebabs

Enjoy your kebabs with a lovely hot baked potato.

Ingredients

- ½ yellow pepper
- 4 long rosemary stalks (they need to be woody)
- 8 cherry tomatoes
- 8 cooked cocktail sausages
- 1 tablespoon runny honey
- 1 tablespoon wholegrain mustard

Equipment

- workmat
- tablespoon
- scissors
- cup
- pastry brush
- baking tray
- baking paper
- oven gloves (for adult use)

Serves 2

What to do

1 Line the baking tray with baking paper.

2 Break up the pepper into 8 big pieces.

3 Trim one end of each rosemary stalk at an angle carefully with the scissors to make a point, then pull off all but the very end leaves to make 8 kebab sticks. (Remember, when using scissors, 'everyone knows, it's best to point them at your toes'!)

KATY SAYS
Vegetarian sausages or cooked pieces of chicken also taste delicious.

4 Assemble the kebabs by threading the pepper, tomatoes and sausages on to the rosemary stalks. Make 4 colourful kebabs with the ingredients. Put the finished kebabs on the baking tray.

5 Make the sticky topping by mixing the honey and mustard together in the cup. Brush the kebabs with the sticky topping.

6 You'll need to ask an adult for help with this part. Place in a preheated oven, 180°C fan, 200°C, Gas Mark 6, for 15–20 minutes.

Once your Sausage Kebabs have cooled down a little, you can eat them!

Before cooking, wash your hands and put an apron on

i can cook

Tea

Carrot & courgette muffins

Serve 1 or 2 muffins with a glass of diluted orange juice or some berries.

Ingredients
- 1 courgette (about 20 g)
- 1 carrot (about 20 g)
- 1 egg
- 2 tablespoons milk
- 1 heaped tablespoon raisins
- 1 tablespoon sunflower or vegetable oil
- 75 g plain flour
- 15 g light soft brown sugar
- 1 level teaspoon baking powder

Equipment
- workmat
- scales
- tablespoon
- 2 teaspoons
- multi-purpose grater
- 2 mixing bowls
- fork
- mini muffin tray
- 9 mini muffin cases
- baking tray
- oven gloves (for adult use)

Makes 9 mini muffins

What to do

1 Line 9 of the muffin tray holes with the muffin cases.

2 Snap the courgette, then carefully grate it. Snap the carrot, then carefully grate that too. Break the egg into a bowl and whisk it with a fork. Add the grated courgette, grated carrot, raisins, milk and the oil and mix. This is called the wet bowl.

3 In the other bowl, mix together the flour, sugar and baking powder. This is called the dry bowl.

4 Pour the wet bowl into the dry bowl and give it a good stir with the tablespoon.

5 Using the 2-spoon method with the teaspoons, spoon the mixture into the muffin cases in the muffin tray.

6 Place the muffin tray on the baking tray. You'll need to ask an adult for help with this part. Place the tray in a preheated oven, 200°C fan, 220°C, Gas Mark 7, for 12–15 minutes.

Once the Carrot and Courgette Muffins have cooled down a little, you can eat them!

Italian cOrn bread

Serve a slice with carrot and cucumber batons.

Ingredients

- 1 dessertspoon olive oil, plus some for greasing
- 50 g plain flour
- 50 g polenta (quick cook, dried)
- 1 teaspoon baking powder
- pinch of pepper
- 50 g soft goat's cheese (without a rind)
- handful of fresh basil leaves, torn
- 1 dessertspoon grated Parmesan cheese
- pinch of dried chilli flakes (not too much!)
- 1 egg
- 100 ml buttermilk

Equipment

- workmat
- scales
- measuring jug
- teaspoon
- dessertspoon
- pastry brush
- mixing bowl
- fork
- cup
- spatula
- small loaf tin (500 g/ 1 lb size)
- baking tray
- oven gloves (for adult use)

Makes 5–6 slices

What to do

1 Brush the inside of the loaf tin with a little olive oil and put it on the baking tray.

2 Put the flour, polenta, baking powder and pepper in the bowl and mix together with the fork.

3 Use your fingers to crumble the goat's cheese into the dry ingredients, then stir.

4 Tear the basil leaves into small pieces and add these, along with the Parmesan and chilli flakes.

5 Break the egg into the cup and mix with the fork. In the measuring jug, put the buttermilk and olive oil in together and add the egg. Stir well.

6 Add the egg mix to the dry bowl and stir quickly but well, making sure there are no dry bits. Put the mixture in the loaf tin – the spatula will help you get it all out of the bowl.

7 You'll need to ask an adult for help with this part. Place in a preheated oven, 200°C fan, 220°C, Gas Mark 7, for 20–25 minutes until golden on the top.

Once the Italian Corn Bread has cooled down, carefully cut it into slices and eat it!

Tomato spirals

Eat 2 each with some salad
for a healthy snack.

Ingredients

- vegetable oil for greasing
- flour for dusting
- 125 g puff pastry (at room temperature)
- 2 level dessertspoons tomato purée
- 30 g grated Cheddar cheese
- 4 fresh basil leaves

Equipment

- workmat
- scales
- dessertspoon
- grater
- pastry brush
- flour dredger
- rolling pin
- butter knife
- baking tray
- baking paper
- oven gloves (for adult use)

What to do

Makes about 12 spirals

1 Line the baking tray with baking paper and brush it with a little vegetable oil.

2 Sprinkle your workmat with a little flour from the dredger. Roll out the pastry into a big rectangle until it's about 3 mm thick. Use the knife to spread a thin layer of tomato purée all over the pastry – make sure you spread it right to the edges.

3 Sprinkle the grated Cheddar on top. Tear the basil leaves with your fingers and scatter them on to the pastry, tomato and cheese.

4 Roll up the pastry into a long sausage shape, hiding all the filling inside.

5 Carefully cut the pastry roll into slices with the knife, and lay the slices on the baking tray so you can see the spiral. Sometimes the pastry gets squashed when you cut it, so use your fingers gently to squeeze the spirals back to a round (Swiss roll) shape.

6 You'll need to ask an adult for help with this part. Place the spirals in a preheated oven, 200°C fan, 220°C, Gas Mark 7, for 15 minutes.

Once the Tomato Spirals have cooled down a little, you can eat them!

Cheese & cress muffins

Serve 1 or 2 warm muffins each, with soup.

Ingredients

- 120 g plain flour
- 1 teaspoon baking powder
- pinch of dry mustard powder
- small bunch (about 1 tablespoon) salad cress
- 20 g feta cheese
- 20 g grated Cheddar cheese
- 1 tablespoon grated hard Italian cheese, like Parmesan
- 1 egg (you'll only need the white part)
- 3 tablespoons vegetable oil
- 3 tablespoons milk
- pinch of pepper

Equipment

- workmat
- scales
- 2 teaspoons
- tablespoon
- 2 mixing bowls
- scissors
- 2 cups
- fork or whisk
- mini muffin tray
- 12 mini muffin cases
- baking tray
- oven gloves (for adult use)

Makes 12 mini muffins

What to do

1 Line the muffin tray with the muffin cases.

2 Put the flour, baking powder and mustard powder in a bowl and mix together. 'Harvest' the salad cress using clean scissors, then chop it up in a cup and add it to the flour bowl. (Remember, when using scissors, 'everyone knows, it's best to point them at your toes'!) Use a fork to smash the feta cheese on the mat, then add it to the bowl. Add the other cheeses, season with pepper and mix well. This is called the dry bowl.

3 Break the egg into a cup. Place your hand over the other bowl and pour the egg into your hand letting the white run through your fingers while you hold on to the yolk in the palm of your hand (keep the yolk for another recipe). Whisk the egg white with a fork or whisk until it's bubbly. Add the oil and milk and mix well. This is called the wet bowl.

4 Add the wet bowl to the dry bowl and stir with the fork until just combined. Use the 2 teaspoons to spoon the mixture into the muffin cases by the 2-spoon method (see page 7).

5 Place the muffin tray on the baking tray. You'll need to ask an adult to help with this part. Bake in a preheated oven, 200°C fan, 220°C, Gas Mark 7, for 12–15 minutes or until puffed and golden.

KATY SAYS
Try using some chopped rocket instead of cress for a different flavour.

Cool the muffins in the tray for 5 minutes, then remove them and cool on wire racks. Once they have cooled, you can eat them!

Savoury bites

Serve with vegetable soup and apple slices for a healthy snack.

Makes 6–8 bites

Ingredients
- 100 g self-raising flour
- 25 g soft butter
- 5 chive stems
- 25 g feta cheese
- 50 ml whole milk

Equipment
- workmat
- scales
- measuring jug
- mixing bowl
- cup
- scissors
- fork
- flour dredger
- rolling pin
- cutter
- baking tray
- baking paper
- oven gloves (for adult use)

What to do

1 Line the baking tray with baking paper.

2 Put the flour and butter in the bowl and rub them together with your fingers until the mixture becomes crumbly (just imagine you are tickling it!).

3 Put the chives in the cup and chop with clean scissors. (Remember, when using scissors, 'everyone knows, it's best to point them at your toes'!) Add to the bowl. Crumble the feta cheese using a fork or your fingers and add to the bowl too. Stir with the fork.

4 Pour most of the milk into the mixture and stir it with the fork until it all sticks together (you may need to add a little more of the milk if it's dry). Shape the dough with your hands into a ball.

5 Sprinkle a little flour onto your workmat. Squash the mixture with your hands, or roll it with the rolling pin, until it is about 5 mm thick (remember, the flour will rise in the oven so the bites will get bigger.)

6 Using a cutter, gently cut out shapes and put them on the baking tray. You'll need to ask an adult for help with this part. Place in a preheated oven, 200°C fan, 220°C, Gas Mark 7, for 8–10 minutes until risen and golden on the top.

KATY SAYS
After cutting your first shapes, you can squeeze the dough together and roll it out again to use up all the mixture.

Once the Savoury Bites have cooled down a little, you can eat them!

Olive bread

Serve 1 each with some butter
or with cheese and tomatoes.

**Makes 8
small rolls**

Ingredients
- 250 g bread flour
- ½ teaspoon salt (optional)
- ½ teaspoon white caster sugar
- 1 level teaspoon instant yeast
- 6 green or black olives (without stones) (try in brine or dry versions)
- sprig of fresh rosemary
- 150 ml warm water
- 1 tablespoon olive oil, plus some for greasing

Equipment
- workmat
- scales
- measuring jug
- teaspoon
- tablespoon
- pastry brush
- mixing bowl
- fork
- flour dredger
- tea towel
- baking tray
- oven gloves (for adult use)

What to do

1 Brush the baking tray with a little olive oil.

2 Put the flour, salt (if using), sugar and yeast in the bowl and mix them together with the fork. Tear the olives with your fingers and add them to the bowl. Pull the leaves off the rosemary sprig and add those too. Using your finger, make a hole or dip in the middle of the flour mixture and add the water and oil. Mix it with the fork until it starts to stick together in a ball.

3 Turn the whole bowl of flour and dough on to your mat and squeeze it to make it all stick together. Knead the dough with your fingers by pulling it to stretch and folding it over. Keep doing this until it looks and feels smooth. If it gets sticky, sprinkle a little flour over it. Then put the dough back in the bowl and cover with the clean tea towel. Put it in a warm place for 45–60 minutes so that the yeast works its magic and the dough grows.

4 Tear the dough into chunks and roll it into 8 small balls. Put the rolls on the baking tray.

5 You'll need to ask an adult for help with this part. Place the baking tray in a preheated oven, 210°C fan, 230°C, Gas Mark 8, for around 10 minutes, or until risen and browned on top.

Once the Olive Bread rolls have cooled down a little, you can eat them!

Sunshine muffins

Share a muffin with a glass of diluted fruit juice.

Ingredients

- 1 cup plain wholemeal flour
- 2 tablespoons porridge oats
- 1 tablespoon dark soft brown sugar
- 1½ teaspoons mixed spice
- 2 teaspoons baking powder
- 180–200 g tinned mango (in juice, drained)
- 125 ml natural yogurt
- 2 tablespoons vegetable or sunflower oil
- 1 egg
- 20 g pumpkin seeds

Equipment

- workmat
- scales
- measuring jug
- tin-opener (for adult use)
- tablespoon
- teaspoon
- 2 mixing bowls
- fork
- kitchen paper
- scissors
- kitchen paper
- cup
- muffin tray
- 6 muffin cases
- baking tray
- oven gloves (for adult use)

What to do

Makes 6 muffins

1 Line the muffin tray with the muffin cases.

2 Put the flour and oats in one of the bowls. Add the sugar, mixed spice and baking powder and mix with the fork. This is the dry mix.

KATY SAYS
These are ideal to put in your lunchbox if you have an early start at school.

3 Tip the mango on to some kitchen paper to dry off any juice. Cut the mango into small chunks in the cup using clean scissors. (Remember, when using scissors, 'everyone knows, it's best to point them at your toes'!) Put the mango on top of your dry mix. Don't stir just yet!

4 Put the yogurt and oil in the other bowl. Break the egg into the cup and beat with the fork, then add this to the yogurt and oil and mix together well. This is the wet mix.

5 Pour the wet mix into the dry mix and stir until there is no dry mixture to be seen (it should be a soft mixture).

6 With the tablespoon and teaspoon, use the 2-spoon method (see page 7) to fill the muffin cases so they all have about the same amount of mixture. Take a pinch of pumpkin seeds and push these on to the top of each muffin.

7 Place the muffin tray on the baking tray. You'll need to ask an adult for help with this part. Place in a preheated oven, 200°C fan, 220°C, Gas Mark 7, for 20–25 minutes until the pumpkin seeds on top are toasted and the muffins are cooked through. Leave to cool in their cases.

Once the Sunshine Muffins have cooled down, you can eat them!

Soda bread

This bread is great eaten with nice warm soup.

Makes 5–6 slices

Ingredients

- 75 g plain flour
- 100 g wholemeal flour
- 25 g oats
- 1½ teaspoons caster sugar
- ½ teaspoon baking soda
- ½ teaspoon salt (optional)
- 2 level tablespoons linseeds
- 170–180 ml natural yogurt

Equipment

- workmat
- scales
- measuring jug
- teaspoon
- tablespoon
- mixing bowl
- fork
- flour dredger
- butter knife
- pastry brush
- baking tray
- baking paper
- oven gloves (for adult use)

What to do

1 Line the baking tray with baking paper.

2 Put the 2 types of flour and the oats in the bowl and stir together with the fork. Add the sugar, baking soda and salt (if using), and stir. Add the linseeds and stir again.

3 Add most of the yogurt (you may not need it all). You want a soft dough that's not too wet. Stir with the fork until the mixture starts to come together.

KATY SAYS
I take homemade soda bread on my picnics wrapped in a clean tea towel.

4 Sprinkle flour on to your workmat, then tip the dough out on to the mat and form it into a ball with your hands.

5 Put the dough on the baking tray and flatten it slightly with your hand. Mark an X on the top using the knife. Brush the top with yogurt.

6 You'll need to ask an adult for help with this part. Place in a preheated oven, 200°C fan, 220°C, Gas Mark 7, for 20–25 minutes until golden on the top.

Once the Soda Bread has cooled down, carefully cut it into slices and eat it!

Honey tea loaf

Serve a slice with a glass of milk or diluted orange juice for a lovely snack.

Ingredients
- vegetable oil for greasing
- 100 g mixed dried fruit
- 70 ml warm decaffeinated tea (get an adult to make the tea with boiling water)
- 2 tablespoons honey
- 1 egg
- 150 g plain flour
- 1 level teaspoon baking powder
- ½ teaspoon mixed spice

Equipment
- workmat
- scales
- measuring jug
- tablespoon
- teaspoon
- pastry brush
- 2 mixing bowls
- cup
- fork
- small loaf tin (500 g/ 1 lb size)
- baking tray
- oven gloves (for adult use)

Makes 6–8 slices

What to do

1 Brush the inside of the loaf tin with vegetable oil and put it on the baking tray.

2 Put the dried fruit in one of the bowls, then pour over the warm tea. Add the honey to the tea and fruit (it helps if the tablespoon is warm).

3 Break the egg into the cup and beat it with the fork. Add it to the tea, fruit and honey mixture and give it a stir. This is called the wet mix.

4 In the other bowl, mix together the flour, baking powder and mixed spice. This is called the dry mix.

5 Tip the wet mix into the dry mix. Stir it together until the mixture becomes thick and sticky and all the flour is mixed in. Pour the mixture into the tin.

6 You'll need to ask an adult for help with this part. Place in a preheated oven, 160°C fan, 180°C, Gas Mark 4, for 20–25 minutes, or until completely cooked through.

KATY SAYS
I like this warm with vanilla custard for pudding.

Once the Honey Tea Loaf has cooled down, tip it out of the loaf tin. Then carefully cut it into slices and eat it!

Melting moments

These biscuits taste delicious with fresh raspberries.

Ingredients
- 50 g caster sugar
- 100 g soft butter
- 1 egg
- ½ teaspoon vanilla extract
- 125 g self-raising flour
- 70 g oats

Equipment
- workmat
- scales
- teaspoon
- mixing bowl
- wooden spoon
- cup
- fork
- plate
- baking tray
- baking paper
- oven gloves (for adult use)

What to do

Makes 6 biscuits

1 Line the baking tray with baking paper.

2 Put the sugar and butter in the bowl and mix them with the wooden spoon until fluffy.

KATY SAYS
You can also make these biscuits with gluten-free flour.

3 Break the egg into the cup, whisk with a fork and add just half of it to the butter mix. Beat it with the wooden spoon.

4 Add the vanilla extract and the flour and mix all the ingredients together until all the flour has disappeared and the mixture is sticky.

5 Divide the dough into 6 lumps and roll them into even-sized balls.

6 Put the oats on a plate, then roll the balls in the oats and put them on the baking tray. Squash the balls slightly with your hands.

7 You'll need to ask an adult for help with this part. Put the baking tray in a preheated oven, 160°C fan, 180°C, Gas Mark 4, for 12–15 minutes or until cooked.

Leave the Melting Moments on the baking tray to cool down, and then you can eat them!

Chunky banana bread

Serve warm with yogurt and fruit as a pudding, or eat as a snack with a glass of milk.

Ingredients

- 1 ripe banana
- 3 dessertspoons sunflower or vegetable oil, plus a little for greasing
- 50 g golden caster sugar
- 110 g plain flour
- 1 level teaspoon baking powder
- 1 egg
- 3 rounded dessertspoons raisins
- 1 teaspoon vanilla extract

Equipment

- workmat
- scales
- dessertspoon
- teaspoon
- pastry brush
- 2 mixing bowls
- fork
- cup
- small loaf tin (500 g/ 1 lb size)
- baking tray
- oven gloves (for adult use)

Makes 6–8 slices

What to do

1 Brush the inside of the loaf tin with the oil and put it on the baking tray.

2 Peel the banana and put it in one of the bowls. Use the fork to mash the banana up, then add 3 dessertspoons of oil and mix. This is called the wet bowl.

3 Put the sugar, flour and baking powder in the other bowl, and stir them together. This is called the dry bowl.

4 Break the egg in the cup and beat with the fork, then add it to the wet bowl. Add the raisins and vanilla extract to the wet bowl and stir all the wet ingredients together. Tip the wet bowl into the dry bowl and give it all a good stir.

5 Pour the mixture into the loaf tin. You'll need to ask an adult for help with this part. Place in a preheated oven, 180°C fan, 200°C, Gas Mark 6, for 30–40 minutes, or until completely cooked through.

Once the Chunky Banana Bread has cooled down, carefully cut it into slices and eat it!

Gold digger buns

Eat a bun with some fresh grapes for a lovely fruity treat.

Ingredients
- 6 dried 'ready-to-eat' apricots
- 60 g butter
- 110 g self-raising flour
- 30 g caster sugar
- 1 egg

Equipment
- workmat
- scales
- scissors
- mixing bowl
- fork
- cup
- flour dredger
- baking tray
- baking paper
- oven gloves (for adult use)

What to do

Makes 5–6 buns

1 Line the baking tray with baking paper.

2 Cut up the apricots with clean scissors. (Remember, when using scissors, 'everyone knows, it's best to point them at your toes'!)

3 Put the butter and flour into the bowl and rub them together with your fingers until the mixture becomes crumbly (just imagine you are tickling it!). Add the chopped apricots and sugar to the bowl and mix in with the fork.

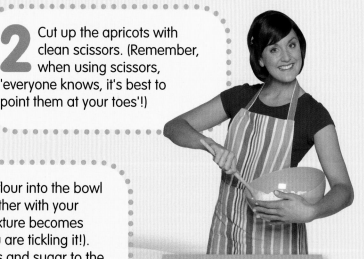

KATY SAYS
Take these on a play-date to share with friends.

4 Break the egg into a cup and whisk it with the fork. Add the whisked egg to the mixture in the bowl and stir until it becomes a soft dough. If it's too sticky, you can add some more flour.

5 Sprinkle flour on the workmat, then put the dough on top. Divide the dough into 6 even-sized pieces and put them on the baking tray.

6 You'll need to ask an adult for help with this part. Place the tray in a preheated oven, 160°C fan, 180°C, Gas Mark 4, for 15–20 minutes.

Leave your Gold Digger Buns to cool down on the baking tray, and then you can eat them!

Fresh fruit flapjacks

Serve the flapjacks with some extra fresh fruit.

Ingredients
- 80 g blueberries or other soft fruit
- 35 g oats
- 35 g wholemeal flour
- 25 g caster sugar
- 25 g butter, plus extra for greasing

Equipment
- workmat
- scales
- fork
- plate
- mixing bowl
- small loaf tin (500 g/ 1 lb size)
- baking tray
- oven gloves (for adult use)

Serves 4

What to do

1 Grease the inside of the loaf tin with a little butter, using your fingers.

2 Squash the blueberries with the back of a fork on a plate. These will go in the middle of the flapjack.

KATY SAYS
I like making these with different fruits – fresh raspberry ones are delicious.

3 Put the oats, flour, sugar and butter in the bowl and rub them together with your fingers until the mixture becomes crumbly (just imagine you are tickling it!).

4 Put half the crumbly mixture in the tin and press it down firmly with your hand. Spread the squashed blueberries evenly on top with your fingers.

5 Pour the remaining crumbly mixture on top to hide the blueberries and pat it down all over, so that it's firm but not hard.

6 Put the tin on the baking tray. You'll need to ask an adult for help with this part. Bake in a preheated oven, 160°C fan, 180°C, Gas Mark 4, for about 20 minutes.

Let the Fresh Fruit Flapjack cool down completely before tipping it out and cutting into 4 slices. Then you can eat it!

Katy's shortbread

Serve 1 or 2 each with some fresh fruit and a glass of milk for a healthy snack.

Ingredients
- 60 g plain flour
- 40 g butter (room temperature)
- ½ teaspoon vanilla extract
- 20 g caster sugar
- 6 glacé cherries

Equipment
- workmat
- scales
- teaspoon
- mixing bowl
- scissors
- wooden spoon
- flour dredger
- rolling pin
- cutter
- baking tray
- baking paper
- oven gloves (for adult use)

What to do

Makes about 8 biscuits

1 Line the baking tray with baking paper.

2 Put the flour and butter in the bowl and rub them together with your fingers until the mixture becomes crumbly (just imagine you are tickling it!).

3 Add the vanilla extract to the bowl and mix in the caster sugar. Cut the cherries into small pieces with clean scissors. (Remember, when using scissors, 'everyone knows, it's best to point them at your toes'!) Add these to the mixing bowl and stir it all up with the wooden spoon.

KATY SAYS
Make these biscuits as a lovely gift for someone special.

4 Squeeze the mixture into a ball with your hands until it all sticks together. Sprinkle a clean surface with flour, then roll the dough out flat with a rolling pin until it's about 5 mm thick.

5 Use the cutter to cut shapes out of your mixture and place them on the baking tray. You can roll the dough out again to cut more shortbread biscuits until it is all used up.

6 You'll need to ask an adult for help with this part. Place the baking tray in a pre-heated oven, 160°C fan, 180°C, Gas Mark 4, for 15–20 minutes.

Once the biscuits have cooled down you can eat them, but not all at once!

Fruit & fudge buns

Serve 1 each with a glass of fruit juice.

Makes 4 buns

Ingredients
- butter for greasing
- 150 g white bread flour
- ½ teaspoon salt (optional)
- 1 teaspoon caster sugar
- 1 teaspoon mixed spice
- 3 tablespoons mixed dried fruit
- 2 tablespoons ready-chopped fudge
- 1 teaspoon instant yeast
- 125 ml milk, at room temperature

Equipment
- workmat
- scales
- measuring jug
- teaspoon
- tablespoon
- mixing bowl
- fork
- flour dredger
- pastry brush
- tea towel
- muffin tray
- baking tray
- oven gloves (for adult use)

What to do

1 Wipe a little butter round the inside of 4 of the holes in the muffin tray with your fingers.

KATY SAYS
I sometimes use chocolate drops instead of fudge.

2 Put the flour, salt (if using), sugar and mixed spice in the bowl and mix together with the fork. Add the dried fruit and fudge and stir. Add the instant yeast to the flour mix and stir.

3 Make a dip in the middle of the flour mix and pour in some but not all of the milk (you may not need it all). Stir it together until it starts to stick together in a ball.

4 Turn the dough on to your workmat and start to squeeze it to make it all stick together. Knead the dough with your fingers by pulling it to stretch and folding it over and repeating. Keep kneading the dough until it looks and feels smooth. If it gets too sticky, sprinkle a little flour on it.

5 Divide the dough into 4 lumps by pulling it apart and push one into each of the muffin holes. Cover with the clean tea towel and put in a warm place for about 45–60 minutes so that the yeast works its magic and the buns increase in size.

6 Place the muffin tray on the baking tray. You'll need to ask an adult for help with this part. Place in a preheated oven, 180°C fan, 200°C, Gas Mark 6, for 20–25 minutes until risen and golden. Remove the buns from the tin while they are still warm.

Once the Fruit and Fudge Buns have cooled down a little, you can eat them!

Marmalade cake

Enjoy a slice of cake with a glass of milk.

Ingredients
- vegetable oil for greasing
- 100 g self-raising flour
- 50 g soft butter
- 50 g caster sugar
- ½ teaspoon mixed spice
- 1 generous tablespoon marmalade
- 1 tablespoon orange juice
- 50 g raisins
- 1–2 tablespoons milk
- 1 teaspoon demerara sugar

Equipment
- workmat
- scales
- teaspoon
- tablespoon
- pastry brush
- 2 mixing bowls
- fork
- spatula
- small loaf tin (500 g/ 1 lb size)
- baking tray
- oven gloves (for adult use)

What to do

Makes 6 slices

1 Brush some oil around the inside of the loaf tin and put it on the baking tray.

2 Put the flour and butter in a bowl and rub them together with your fingers until the mixture becomes crumbly (just imagine you are tickling it!).

3 Add the caster sugar and mixed spice to the flour and stir well with the fork. This is the dry mix.

4 Spoon the marmalade into the other bowl. Add the orange juice, raisins and 1 tablespoon of milk and mix well with the fork. This is the wet mix.

5 Pour the wet mix into the dry mix and stir until there is no dry mix to be seen (it should be a soft mixture). Add a little more milk if it's too dry.

6 Put the mixture in the loaf tin – the spatula will help you get all the mixture out of the bowl! Sprinkle the top with the demerara sugar.

KATY SAYS
This is a great recipe if you can't eat eggs.

7 You'll need to ask an adult for help with this part. Place in a preheated oven, 160°C fan, 180°C, Gas Mark 4, for 30–35 minutes or until risen and golden.

Once the Marmalade Cake has cooled down a little, you can slice it and eat it!

Blackberry bites

Serve these sweet scones with extra blackberries or with yogurt on the top.

Ingredients
- 125 g self-raising flour
- 25 g butter
- 25 g caster sugar
- 50 g (about 16) blackberries
- 100 ml buttermilk

Equipment
- workmat
- scales
- measuring jug
- mixing bowl
- fork
- flour dredger
- cutter
- baking tray
- baking paper
- oven gloves
  (for adult use)

What to do

Makes 6–10 depending on size of cutter (portion 1–2 bites)

1 Line the baking tray with baking paper.

3 Add the buttermilk gradually (this is important, as you may not need it all) and stir until the mixture starts to stick together.

2 Put the flour and butter in the bowl and rub them together with your fingers until the mixture becomes crumbly (just imagine you are tickling it!). Stir in the sugar. Add the blackberries and gently mix into the crumbly mixture with the fork (try to keep the blackberries whole).

KATY SAYS
If you don't have blackberries, blueberries are really tasty too.

4 Sprinkle flour on to the workmat. Turn the dough out on to the mat and gently form it into a ball. Gently flatten the dough with your hands until it's about 1.5 cm thick.

5 Use the cutter to cut out the scones and put them on the baking tray.

6 You'll need to ask an adult to help with this part. Place in a preheated oven, 200°C fan, 220°C, Gas Mark 7, for 10–12 minutes until golden on the top.

Once the Blackberry Bites have cooled down, you can eat them!

Fruity fromage frais cake

Serve a slice of this fruity cake with a drink.

Ingredients
- 1 egg
- 45 g pot fruity fromage frais (any flavour)
- 1 fresh peach or nectarine
- 3 pots self-raising flour (use the empty fromage frais pot to measure)
- ½ pot caster sugar
- 2 tablespoons vegetable oil, plus some for greasing

Equipment
- workmat
- scales
- tablespoon
- pastry brush
- mixing bowl
- fork
- butter knife
- small loaf tin (500 g/ 1 lb size)
- baking tray
- oven gloves (for adult use)

Makes 6–8 slices

What to do

1 Brush the inside of the loaf tin with vegetable oil and put it on the baking tray.

2 Break the egg into the bowl and beat it with a fork. Add the fromage frais, then wash out and dry the pot.

3 Using your knife, very carefully 'take it for a walk' around the peach, cutting down to the stone hidden inside. Then twist the 2 halves to open it up. Cut the peach flesh into small bite-sized pieces and add to the bowl.

4 Add the self-raising flour, sugar and vegetable oil and stir it all together until there are no dry bits and the mixture is smooth and creamy. Put the cake mixture in the loaf tin.

5 You'll need to ask an adult for help with this part. Place in a preheated oven, 160°C fan, 180°C, Gas Mark 4, for 25–30 minutes or until cooked and golden brown.

KATY SAYS
Using the fromage frais pot to measure other ingredients is very clever!

Once the Fruity Fromage Frais Cake has cooled down, carefully cut it into slices and eat it!

Before cooking, wash your hands and put an apron on

i can cook

Sweet treats

chocolate & mandarin pudding

Eat a quarter of the pudding with some of the leftover tinned mandarins.

Ingredients
- 2 heaped teaspoons instant hot chocolate powder, plus 1 level teaspoon, to sprinkle
- 50 ml warm water
- 7 sponge fingers
- 16 mandarin segments (tinned or fresh)
- 75 g cream cheese
- 125 g natural yogurt
- ½ teaspoon vanilla extract

Equipment
- workmat
- scales
- measuring jug
- tin-opener (for adult use)
- 2 teaspoons
- mixing bowl
- small spring whisk
- clear trifle bowl (about 400 ml capacity)

Serves 4

What to do

KATY SAYS
I also make this using juicy fresh oranges.

1 Mix the chocolate powder with the warm water in the measuring jug.

2 Put a layer of sponge fingers (half of them) in the bottom of the trifle bowl and pour half of the drinking chocolate mix on top. Arrange 8 mandarin segments on top of the sponge fingers.

3 Put the cream cheese in the mixing bowl and whisk until smooth. Add the yogurt and the vanilla extract and whisk again. Spoon half of the creamy cheesy mix into the trifle bowl, hiding the mandarins and sponge fingers.

4 Add another layer of all the ingredients, starting with the remaining sponge fingers. Then pour over the remaining chocolate drink and add the remaining mandarins. Finally spoon over the remaining cheesy mix just like you did before.

5 Sprinkle 1 teaspoon of chocolate powder on the top, cover and place in the fridge for about 1 hour.

Once the Chocolate and Mandarin Pudding has set, you can eat it!

Lemon & lime cheesecakes

Serve with some fresh fruit such as raspberries.

Ingredients
- 2 oaty digestive-style biscuits
- 2 dessertspoons melted butter (get an adult to melt it for you)
- 1 lemon
- 1 lime
- 125 g mascarpone cheese
- 1 level tablespoon icing sugar

Equipment
- workmat
- scales
- dessertspoon
- tablespoon
- greaseproof paper bag
- rolling pin
- 2 mixing bowls
- sharp knife and cutting mat (for adult use)
- fork
- 2 teaspoons
- 2 small glass pots or ramekins

What to do

Serves 2

KATY SAYS
If you don't have a greaseproof bag, you can crush the biscuits in a bowl using the end of a rolling pin.

1 Place the biscuits in the grease-proof bag and use a rolling pin to bash them gently until they are crushed up into crumbs.

2 Put the crushed biscuits in a bowl, pour in the melted butter and mix well with the dessert-spoon. The crumbs will change colour as they soak up the butter.

3 Spoon the crumbs into the bottom of each of the glass pots and press the mixture down firmly with your fingers to make a biscuit base.

4 Take a lemon and roll it on the table top, pressing down firmly to loosen the juice inside. Do the same with a lime. Ask an adult to cut the lemon and lime in half. Squeeze the juice from half of each fruit into the other bowl.

5 Add the mascarpone cheese and icing sugar and mix them together with the juice using a fork.

6 Using the 2 teaspoons and the 2-spoon method (see page 7), spoon the cheesy mixture into the dishes to hide the biscuit bases. Cover the pots and put them in the fridge for 2 hours.

Once the Lemon & Lime Cheesecakes have set, you can eat them!

Strawberry meringue ice cream

Serve the ice cream with some fresh berries such as blackberries or blueberries.

Ingredients
- 125 ml double cream
- 2 heaped dessertspoons natural yogurt
- 2 level dessertspoons icing sugar
- 4 large strawberries
- 1 meringue nest

Equipment
- workmat
- measuring jug
- dessertspoon
- mixing bowl
- spring whisk or 2 forks
- small plate
- freezerproof container with lid (about 400 ml capacity)

Serves 4

What to do

1 Whisk the cream in the bowl until it's light and fluffy. If you don't have a whisk, you can use 2 forks held together. Add the yogurt and icing sugar to the cream and whisk it again.

2 Place the strawberries on the plate and mash them with the back of a fork until they are squishy. Pull out any green stalks. Tip the mashed strawberries into the cream mix.

4 Pour the mixture into the container, put the lid on and put it in the freezer for at least 2 hours or preferably overnight.

3 Hold a meringue nest over the bowl and crush it in your hand, then drop it into the mixture and give it a gentle stir.

KATY SAYS
Homemade ice cream should be taken out of the freezer and put in the fridge about 30 minutes before serving.

Once the Strawberry Meringue Ice Cream has frozen, you can eat it!

Banana & blueberry ice cream

Serve with extra blueberries or wafer biscuits.

Ingredients
- 125 g mascarpone, at room temperature
- 60 g icing sugar
- 20 g blueberries (about 12)
- 1 lemon (ask an adult to cut it in half)
- 1 ripe banana

Equipment
- workmat
- mixing bowl
- tablespoon
- fork
- freezerproof container with lid (such as a 500 g margarine pot)

Serves 4

What to do

KATY SAYS
Eat the ice cream within 3 days – if it lasts that long!

1 Put the mascarpone and sugar in the bowl and mix together with the tablespoon. Gently stir the blueberries into the mixture.

2 Using the fork to help you, squeeze as much lemon juice out of the lemon halves as you can into the mixture and stir.

3 On your workmat, squash the banana with the fork to make sticky mash. Add the mashed banana to the bowl with the mascarpone. Mix with the fork or spoon.

4 Put the mixture in the container and place in the freezer for at least 2 hours.

Once the Banana & Blueberry Ice Cream has frozen, put it in the fridge for 30 minutes to soften slightly, and then you can eat it!

Spiced banana pudding

Eat this pudding with natural yogurt or ice cream and berries.

Ingredients

- 20 g butter, plus extra for greasing
- 2 slices day-old brown bread
- 1 egg
- 125 ml whole milk
- 20 g demerara sugar, plus another teaspoon to sprinkle
- pinch of cinnamon
- 1 ripe small banana
- 1 heaped tablespoon sultanas, raisins or mixed dried fruit

Equipment

- workmat
- scales
- measuring jug
- tablespoon
- butter knife
- cup
- fork
- ovenproof dish (about 400 ml capacity)
- baking tray
- oven gloves (for adult use)

Serves 4

What to do

1 Grease the oven-proof dish with some butter, using your fingers.

2 With the knife, spread one side of each piece of bread with the remaining butter. Cut each slice from corner to corner to make 4 triangles, making 8 in total. Put these to one side.

KATY SAYS
If no-one is eating the over-ripe bananas, use them for this scrumptious spiced banana pudding.

3 Break an egg into the mug and whisk it using a fork. Add the milk, sugar and cinnamon and whisk it again.

4 Peel the banana and carefully cut it into slices with the butter knife.

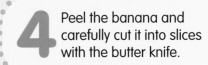

5 Put half of the bread (4 pieces) in the ovenproof dish, add the bananas and sultanas. Then put the remaining bread on top, hiding the banana and fruit.

6 Pour over the egg mixture, sprinkle the extra sugar on top and put the dish on the baking tray.

7 You'll need to ask an adult for help with this part. Place in a preheated oven, 160°C fan, 180°C, Gas Mark 4, for 20–25 minutes, or until completely cooked through.

Once the Spiced Banana Pudding has cooled down a little, you can eat it!

Spiced banana pudding **109**

Baked crumble nectarines

Serve this delicious pudding with natural yogurt.

Ingredients
- 2 tablespoons orange juice
- 40 g plain flour
- 20 g butter
- 10 g demerara sugar
- 20 g oats
- 1 fresh, ripe nectarine

Equipment
- workmat
- scales
- tablespoon
- mixing bowl
- butter knife
- ovenproof dish (about 400 ml capacity)
- baking tray
- oven gloves (for adult use)

Serves 2

What to do

1 Place the dish on the baking tray and pour the orange juice into it.

2 Put the flour and butter in the bowl and rub them together with your fingers until the mixture becomes crumbly (just imagine you are tickling it!). Stir in the demerara sugar (this will give the topping some crunch) and the oats.

3 Split the nectarine into 2 halves by taking the knife 'for a walk' around the fruit. Start at the top where the stalk was and cut all the way around down to the bottom and back up, making sure the blade touches the stone inside as you go round. Twist the 2 halves of the nectarine in opposite directions and they should come apart. Pull the stone out of the centre and lay the 2 halves with their flat sides up in the dish.

KATY SAYS
If you don't have a nectarine, try using a peach instead.

4 Sprinkle the crumble topping over the cut surface of the nectarines.

5 You'll need to ask an adult for help with this part. Place in a preheated oven, 200°C fan, 220°C, Gas Mark 7, for 12–15 minutes until golden on the top.

Once the Baked Crumble Nectarines have cooled down a little, you can eat them!

Bread & butter surprise

Eat the pudding with extra pear pieces and yogurt.

Ingredients

- 25 g soft butter
- 2 slices day-old bread
- 2 tinned pear halves
- 50 g milk chocolate drops
- 1 egg
- ½ cup milk
- 25 g caster sugar

What to do

Equipment

- workmat
- scales
- measuring jug
- tin-opener (for adult use)
- butter knife
- scissors
- dessertspoon
- cup
- fork
- ovenproof dish (about 400 ml capacity)
- baking tray
- oven gloves (for adult use)

Serves 4

1 Grease the inside of the ovenproof dish with a little of the butter, using your fingers.

2 With the knife, spread one side of each piece of bread with the remaining butter. Cut each slice from corner to corner to make 4 triangles, making 8 in total. Put these to one side.

3 Using the scissors or the knife, cut the tinned pear into bite-sized pieces. (Remember, when using scissors, 'everyone knows, it's best to point them at your toes'!) Put these to one side.

4 Arrange a layer of 4 triangles of bread in the bottom of the dish. Sprinkle 2 dessertspoons of the milk chocolate drops over the top, and then some of the chopped pear.

KATY SAYS
I love white chocolate drops in this recipe.

5 Arrange the 4 remaining triangles on top to hide this layer of fruit and chocolate, then sprinkle the top with the remaining chocolate drops and pear pieces. Now break an egg into the cup and stir with the fork. Add the milk and mix well. Add the sugar and stir well, then pour this mixture over the top of the bread layers.

6 Put the dish on the baking tray. You'll need to ask an adult for help with this part. Place in a preheated oven, 180°C fan, 200°C, Gas Mark 6, for 25–30 minutes until golden on the top.

Once the Bread & Butter Surprise has cooled down a little, you can eat it!

Hide & Seek Cheesecakes

These cheesecakes taste great with some extra raspberries.

Ingredients

- 3 digestive biscuits
- 2 dessertspoons melted butter (ask an adult to melt it for you)
- 125 g cream cheese
- 1 egg
- ½ teaspoon vanilla extract
- 30 g caster sugar
- 12 raspberries

Equipment

- workmat
- scales
- teaspoon
- greaseproof paper bag
- rolling pin
- 2 mixing bowls
- 2 dessert-spoons
- cup
- fork
- dessertspoon
- spatula
- 4 small glass pots or ramekins (about 100 ml capacity)
- baking tray
- oven gloves (for adult use)

What to do

Serves 4

1 Place the biscuits in the greaseproof bag and use the rolling pin to bash them gently until they are crushed up into crumbs.

2 Pour the crushed biscuits into a bowl, add the melted butter and stir. Spoon the biscuit mix into the 4 ramekins so that they each get about the same amount. Press down the mixture with your fingers or the back of a spoon to form a base, then put the pots in the fridge.

3 Put the cream cheese in the other bowl. Break the egg into a cup, mix it with a fork, then add it to the cream cheese. Add the vanilla extract and sugar and stir well with the fork.

KATY SAYS
Swap the digestive biscuits for milk chocolate digestive biscuits.

4 Bring the pots back to the workmat and put 3 whole raspberries on to each of the biscuit bases. Using the 2-spoon method with the 2 dessertspoons (see page 7), add some of the cheese mixture to each dish until you have used it all up. The spatula will help you get all the mixture out of the bowl. Put the pots on the baking tray.

5 You'll need to ask an adult to help with this part. Place in a preheated oven, 180°C fan, 200°C, Gas Mark 6, for 20 minutes until lightly golden brown and just set in the middle.

Once the Hide & Seek Cheesecakes have cooled down, you can eat them!

Rhubarb cobbler

This dessert is best eaten
with vanilla ice cream.

Ingredients

- 4 tablespoons light muscovado
  sugar
- 5 tablespoons porridge oats
- 3 tablespoons milk or single
  cream
- 200 g fresh rhubarb
- 3 tablespoons orange juice
- 1 teaspoon demerara sugar

Serves 4

Equipment

- workmat
- scales
- tablespoon
- mixing bowl
- fork
- scissors
- ovenproof
  dish (about
  400 ml
  capacity)
- baking tray
- oven gloves
  (for adult use)

What to do

1 Put 1 tablespoon of the muscovado sugar, the
oats and the enough milk to 'bind' (stick) the
mixture together into the bowl. Mix it all up well
with the fork. This is going to be your cobbler topping.
Put this to one side.

KATY SAYS
Try adding some
grated orange zest –
does it change the
colour and taste?

2 Cut the rhubarb
into small chunks
using clean
scissors and put it in the
bottom of the ovenproof
dish. (Remember, when
using scissors, 'everyone
knows, it's best to point
them at your toes'!)

3 Sprinkle the remaining 3 tablespoons of muscovado sugar over the top. (The sweetness of fresh rhubarb varies, and you can add more sugar if needed once it is cooked.) Pour the orange juice over too.

4 Divide the cobbler topping mix into 4 even-sized lumps, and roll these into balls with your hands. Drop these on top of the rhubarb. Sprinkle with the demerara sugar and put the dish on the baking tray.

5 You'll need to ask an adult to help with this part. Bake in a preheated oven, 180°C fan, 200°C, Gas Mark 6, for 20–25 minutes or until the rhubarb is soft.

Once the Rhubarb Cobbler has cooled down, you can eat it!

Banana & toffee pudding

You'll enjoy this with plenty of custard.

Ingredients
- vegetable oil for greasing
- 2 tablespoons ready-made toffee sauce
- 1 banana
- 70 g self-raising flour
- 70 g soft butter
- 70 g caster sugar
- 1 egg
- ½ teaspoon mixed spice

Equipment
- workmat
- scales
- tablespoon
- teaspoon
- pastry brush
- butter knife
- mixing bowl
- wooden spoon
- spatula
- cup
- ovenproof dish (about 400 ml capacity)
- baking tray
- oven gloves (for adult use)

What to do

Serves 4

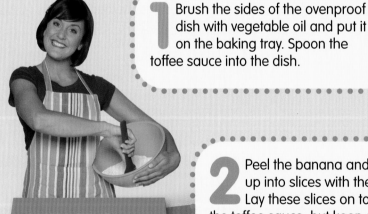

1 Brush the sides of the ovenproof dish with vegetable oil and put it on the baking tray. Spoon the toffee sauce into the dish.

KATY SAYS
You can change the toffee sauce for chocolate sauce!

2 Peel the banana and cut it up into slices with the knife. Lay these slices on top of the toffee sauce, but keep some back for the top of the pudding!

3 Put the flour, butter, sugar and egg in the bowl and beat them together with the wooden spoon until smooth. Add the mixed spice and beat again. Put the mixture on top of the banana and toffee. The spatula will help you get it all out. Scatter the rest of the banana over the top.

4 You'll need to ask an adult for help with this part. Place in a preheated oven, 160°C fan, 180°C, Gas Mark 4, for 25–30 minutes or until risen and golden.

Once the Banana & Toffee Pudding has cooled down a little, you can eat it!

Katy's apricot tarts

Serve 1 each with yogurt and the leftover apricots.

Makes 4
warning: contains nuts

Ingredients
- 12 tinned apricot halves
- flour for sprinkling
- 250 g fresh puff pastry
- 125 g marzipan
- 4 teaspoons raspberry jam

Equipment
- workmat
- scales
- tin-opener (for adult use)
- 2 teaspoons
- kitchen paper
- flour dredger
- rolling pin
- large cutter (98 mm)
- medium cutter (78 mm)
- scissors
- baking tray
- baking paper
- oven gloves (for adult use)

What to do

1 Line the baking tray with baking paper. Put the apricot halves on kitchen paper to dry.

2 Sprinkle flour on the workmat and then roll out the puff pastry into a large rectangle – is it big enough to cut out the 4 bigger circles? Cut out the circles with the large cutter. Take the smaller cutter and press this down into the large pastry circles – try not to cut all the way through. Put these 4 pastry circles on the baking tray.

3 Roll out the marzipan so it is big enough to cut out 4 of the smaller circles (you may need to sprinkle a little more flour on the workmat to stop the marzipan from sticking). Cut out the marzipan circles and put these on top of the pastry circles.

4 Place half an apricot in the centre of each marzipan circle. Using clean scissors, cut the rest of the apricot halves into small pieces and use them to cover the rest of the marzipan, leaving a circle of pastry all around. (Remember, when using scissors, 'everyone knows, it's best to point them at your toes'!)

5 Using the 2-spoon method with the 2 teaspoons (see page 7), drop some raspberry jam over the top of the apricot pieces.

6 You'll need to ask an adult for help with this part. Place in a preheated oven, 200°C fan, 220°C, Gas Mark 7, for 10–15 minutes until the pastry is risen and golden.

Once Katy's Apricot Tarts have cooled down a little, you can eat them!

Apple dappy

Eat 1 spiral each as a snack

Makes 7

Ingredients
- 100 g self-raising flour
- 30 g butter
- 1 tablespoon caster sugar
- 60 ml milk or single cream
- 80 g tinned apples
- pinch of ground cinnamon
- 2 teaspoons demerara sugar

Equipment
- workmat
- scales
- tin-opener (for adult use)
- tablespoon
- teaspoon
- mixing bowl
- fork
- cup
- flour dredger
- rolling pin
- butter knife
- baking tray
- baking paper
- oven gloves (for adult use)

What to do

1 Line the baking tray with baking paper.

2 Put the flour and butter in the bowl and rub them together with your fingers until the mixture becomes crumbly (just imagine you are tickling it!). Stir in the caster sugar using the fork. Add some but not all of the milk or cream and mix until you get a soft dough (you may not need all the milk or cream).

KATY SAYS
This is great recipe to share with your friends.

3 Put the apples in the bottom of the cup. Add the cinnamon and 1 heaped teaspoon of the demerara sugar. Mix well. Use the spoon to chop the apple into smaller pieces.

4 Sprinkle flour on the workmat, then roll out the dough to about 5 mm thick. Try to keep a rectangular shape. Spread the apple mix on top, then roll up like a sausage along the long side.

5 Cut into 7 thick rings using the knife. Place one on the centre of the baking tray, making sure you can see the spiral. Then add the remaining 6 around the outside in a circle, almost touching each other. Sprinkle with the rest of the demerara.

6 You'll need to ask an adult for help with this part. Place in a preheated oven, 200°C fan, 220°C, Gas Mark 7, for 20–25 minutes.

Once the Apple Dappy has cooled down a little, you can eat it!

My recipe gallery

KATY SAYS
Why don't you stick pictures of the recipes you've cooked here?

Index

Acknowledgements

Thank you to the children who cooked for the photography: George Bassirian, Kayne Cadogan, Dexter Godfrey, Stirling Hampton, Jessica Hawkins, Florence Hellier, Maximilian Kuczynski, Sybbi Rhaye Laubscher, Rose Lemon, Isobel McGrath, Duke Minnell-Newton, Paige Robinson, Mabel Sims, Joel Thomas-Bagley, Alastair Thorpe, Amelia Thorpe, Daisy White, Molly White, Bo Williams-Leedham, and Raphael.

Thank you also to Lakeland (www.lakeland.co.uk) for kitchen supplies and www.4yourkitchen.co.uk for the kitchen scales and weights.

Executive Producer: Christopher Pilkington
Presenter: Katy Ashworth
Katy Ashworth's Agent: Jan Croxson
Literary Agent: Amanda Preston
Paralegal: Penny Roberts
Head of Consumer Products: Seema Khan
Licensing Assistant: Nicole Sloman

Group Publisher: Denise Bates
Managing Editor: Clare Churly
Creative Director: Tracy Killick
Designer: Balley Design
Photographer: Vanessa Davies
Home Economist: Denise Smart
Stylist: Liz Hippisley
Production Manager: David Hearn